my people

my people

Oodgeroo

WILEY

Fifth edition published in 2021 by
John Wiley & Sons Australia, Ltd
42 McDougall St, Milton Qld 4064
Office also in Melbourne

Typeset in Garamond Premier Pro Regular 12/15pt by SPi Global, India

First edition 1970
Second edition 1981
Third edition 1990
Fourth edition 2008

ISBN: 978-0-730-39108-1

A catalogue record for this book is available from the National Library of Australia

Cover art by Oodgeroo

Judith Wright, 'Two Dreamtimes' from *Collected Poems*, Judith Wright, HarperCollins Publishers Australia Pty Limited

10 9 8 7 6 5 4 3 2 1

Dedicated to my son Kabul
of the tribe Noonuccal
Custodian of the land Minjerribah
(Vivian Charles Walker)

Contents

All One Race

Black tribe, yellow tribe, red, white or brown,
From where the sun jumps up to where it goes down,
Herrs and pukka-sahibs, demoiselles and squaws,
All one family, so why make wars?
They're not interested in brumby runs,
We don't hanker after Midnight suns;
I'm for all humankind, not colour gibes;
I'm international, and never mind tribes.

Black, white or brown race, yellow race or red,
From the torrid equator to the ice-fields spread,
Monsieurs and senors, lubras and fraus,
All one family, so why family rows?
We're not interested in their igloos,
They're not mad about kangaroos;
I'm international, never mind place;
I'm for humanity, all one race.

Let Us Not Be Bitter

Away with bitterness, my own dark people
Come stand with me, look forward, not back,
For a new time has come for us.
Now we must change, my people. For so long
Time for us stood still; now we know
Life is change, life is progress,
Life is learning things, life is onward.
White men had to learn civilised ways,
Now it is our turn.
Away with bitterness and the bitter past;
Let us try to understand the white man's ways
And accept them as they accept us;
Let us judge white people by the best of their race.
The prejudiced ones are less than we,
We want them no more than they want us.
Let us not be bitter, that is an empty thing,
A maggot in the mind.
The past is gone like our childhood days of old,
The future comes like dawn after the dark,
Bringing fulfilment.

An Appeal

Statesmen, who make the nation's laws,
With power to force unfriendly doors,
Give leadership in this our cause
    That leaders owe.

Writers, who have the nation's ear,
Your pen a sword opponents fear,
Speak of our evils loud and clear
    That all may know.

Unions, who serve democracy,
Guardians of social liberty,
Warm to the justice of our plea,
    And strike your blow.

Churches, who preach the Nazarene,
Be on our side and intervene,
Show us what Christian love can mean
    Who need it so.

The Press, most powerful of all,
On you the underprivileged call:
Right us a wrong and break the thrall
    That keeps us low.

All white well-wishers, in the end
On you our chiefest hopes depend;
Public opinion's our best friend
   To beat the foe.

The Curlew Cried

Three nights they heard the curlew cry.
It is the warning known of old
That tells them one tonight shall die.

Brother and friend, he comes and goes
Out of the Shadow Land to them,
The loneliest voice that earth knows.

He guards the welfare of his own,
He comes to lead each soul away –
To what dim world, what strange unknown?

Who is it that tonight must go:
The old blind one? The cripple child?
Tomorrow all the camp will know.

The poor dead will be less afraid,
Their tribe brother will be with him
When the dread journey must be made.

'Have courage, death is not the end,'
He seems to say. 'Though you must weep,
Death is kindly and is your friend.'

Three nights the curlew cried. Once more
He comes to take the timorous dead –
To what grim change, what ghostly shore?

Note: The curlew was brother of the Aboriginal peoples. He came to warn them of
a coming death by crying near a camp three nights in succession. They believed that
the curlew came to lead the shade of the dead one away to the unknown world.

Sounds Assail Me

Something obscene
In man-made sounds affronts the sweet and clean,
But Nature's never.
Shout of the stormy winds, ever
Toneless and rude, tossing the trees,
The harsh scream of seabirds – these
Somehow belong
As much as the wren's airy song.
Man only, the books tell, knows evil and wrong;
Even as art now the yelp and yell
Like music of hell,
Music made evil, the squawk and squall
When the disc jockeys loose the blare and bawl.
Give me the sounds God made so –
I love them all
Whether loud or low,
From the small, thin
Note of the bee's violin
To the rough sea's uproar,
In wild tumult tumbling upon the shore.

Tree Grave

When our lost one left us
For the Shadow Land,
In bark we bound him,
A weeping band,
And we bore him, wailing
Our wild death croon
To his lonely tree-grave
By the Long Lagoon.

Our wandering fires
Are now far away,
But our thoughts are turning
By night and day
Where he lies for ever
Under the white moon,
By the lit waters
Of the still lagoon.

His hunts are over
And the songs he made;
Poor lonely fellow,
He will be afraid
When the night winds whisper
Their ghostly tune
In the haunted swamp-oaks
By the Long Lagoon.

Dawn Wail for the Dead

Dim light of daybreak now
Faintly over the sleeping camp.
Old lubra first to wake remembers:
First thing every dawn
Remember the dead, cry for them.
Softly at first her wail begins,
One by one as they wake and hear
Join in the cry, and the whole camp
Wails for the dead, the poor dead
Gone from here to the Dark Place:
They are remembered.
Then it is over, life now,
Fires lit, laughter now,
And a new day calling.

Dark Unmarried Mothers

All about the country,
From earliest teens,
Dark unmarried mothers,
Fair game for lechers –
Bosses and station hands,
And in town and city
Low-grade animals
Prowl for safe prey.
Nothing done about it,
No one to protect them –
But hush, you mustn't say so,
Bad taste or something
To challenge the accepted,
Disturbing the established.
Turn the blind eye,
Wash the hands like Pilate.

Consent? Even with consent
It is still seduction.
Is it a white girl?
Then court case and headline
Stern talk of maintenance.
Is it a dark girl?
Then safe immunity;
He takes what he wants
And walks off like a dog.
Was ever even one,

One of all the thousands
Ever made responsible?
For dark unmarried mothers
The law does not run.

No blame for the guilty
But blame uttered only
For anyone made angry
Who dares even mention it,
Challenging old usage,
Established, accepted
And therefore condoned.
Shrug away the problem,
The shame, the injustice;
Turn the blind eye,
Wash the hands like Pilate.

Not My Style

Not my style?
Man! the world will end
And you complain.
I want to do
The things I have not done.
Not just taste the nectar of Gods
But drown in it too.
Shed my grass-root skin.
Emerge!
As woman!
    poet!
        writer!
            musician!

Eat herbs;
Chew grass;
Commit suicide;
Live.
Stuff myself
Of the bitter and the sweet,
Before,
    that thing,
        that thing,
            outside
Comes.

Last of His Tribe

Change is the law. The new must oust the old.
I look at you and am back in the long ago,
Old pinnaroo lonely and lost here,
Last of your clan.
Left only with your memories, you sit
And think of the gay throng, the happy people,
The voices and the laughter
All gone, all gone,
And you remain alone.

I asked and you let me hear
The soft vowelly tongue to be heard now
No more for ever. For me
You enact old scenes, old ways, you who have used
Boomerang and spear.
You singer of ancient tribal songs,
You leader once in the corroboree,
You twice in fierce tribal fights
With wild enemy blacks from over the river,
All gone, all gone. And I feel
The sudden sting of tears, Willie Mackenzie
In the Salvation Army Home.
Displaced person in your own country,
Lonely in teeming city crowds,
Last of your tribe.

Note: Willie Mackenzie was the last surviving member of the Darwarbada tribe of
the Caboolture district. He died in 1968, age unknown, but probably in the
eighties. His tribal name was Geerbo, his totem the native bee. The 'Mackenzie'
came from his family's first white boss, a selector of that name.

The Child Wife

They gave me to an old man,
Joyless and old,
Life's smile of promise
So soon to frown.
Inside his gunya
My childhood over,
I must sit for ever,
And the tears fall down.

It was love I longed for,
Young love like mine,
It was Dunwa wanted me,
The gay and brown.
Oh, old laws that tether me!
Oh, long years awaiting me!
And the grief comes over me,
And the tears fall down.

Happy the small birds
Mating and nesting,
Shrilling their gladness
No grief may drown.
But an old man's gunya
Is my life for ever,
And I think of Dunwa,
And the tears fall down.

The Young Girl Wanda

Crooning her own girl thoughts and dreams
The young girl Wanda,
Grinding nardoo with the women
Softly chanted her simple song
Of all she hated.

'I hate death and the going away,
All sad endings.
I hate things that have no joy,'
Said the young girl Wanda.
'I hate sunset bringing the dark
That is full of secrets,
I hate silence of desolate places,
Swamp-oaks sighing by lonely waters,
And tree graves,'
Said the young girl Wanda.
'I hate old men's rules and laws,
Old wrinkled faces,
The elders who no longer know
What the young know,'
Said the young girl Wanda.

'All time too much hate, you.'
Said the old gin Onah.
'Tell us what you love.'

'I love joy of life,
I love arms around me,
I love life and love,'
Said the young girl Wanda.
'I love all young things,
The young dawn, not the grey day dying,
The white of daybreak on awakening waters.
I love happy things,'
Said the girl Wanda.
'High eagles, the light in eyes we love,
The camp crying for joy when one returns.
I love colour, berries yellow and red,
The grass when it is green,
The blue that is on the kingfisher,
And a bright flower for my black hair,'
Said the young girl Wanda,
'But most of all my strong lover I love,
And his arms around me.'

Whynot Street

Officiously they hawked about
'Petition' to keep abos out,
And slavishly, without a peep,
The feeble yes-men signed like sheep.

And are we still the ousted, then,
And dare you speak for decent men?
This site was ours, you may recall,
Ages before you came at all.

'No abos here!' Why not, Whynot?
And if black-balling and boycott,
First black-ball pride and arrogance,
Boycott this vile intolerance.

White Australia

Since God's good world began,
Not God but godless man
Made barrier and ban,
   And reared each frontier wall.
Brothers, when shall we see
Selfless democracy?
Life is for liberty,
   And earth was made for all.

Let little kiplings rant,
Narrow and arrogant,
Their chauvinistic cant
   That white is nobler birth.
The best of every race
Should here find welcome place;
The colour of his face
   Is no man's test of worth.

Acacia Ridge

White men, turn quickly the earth of Acacia Ridge,
Hide the evidence lying there
Of the black race evicted as of old their fathers were;
Cover up the crime committed this day,
Call it progress, the white man's way.

Take no heed of the pregnant black woman in despair
As with her children she has to go;
Ignore her bitter tears that unheeded flow;
While her children cling to her terrified
Bulldozers huddle the crime aside.

White men, turn quickly the earth of Acacia Ridge,
Plough the guilt in, cover and hide the shame;
These are black and so without right to blame
As bulldozers brutally drive, ruthless and sure
Through and over the poor homes of the evicted poor.

Homeless now they stand and watch as the rain pours down;
This is the injustice brought to the black man there,
Injustice which to whites you would never dare,
You whites with all the power and privilege
Who committed the crime of Acacia Ridge.

The Unhappy Race

The Myall speaks

White fellow, you are the unhappy race.
You alone have left nature and made civilised laws.
You have enslaved yourselves as you enslaved the horse and
other wild things.
Why, white man?
Your police lock up your tribe in houses with bars,
We see poor women scrubbing floors of richer women.
Why, white man, why?
You laugh at 'poor blackfellow', you say we must be like you.
You say we must leave the old freedom and leisure,
We must be civilised and work for you.
Why, white fellow?
Leave us alone, we don't want your collars and ties,
We don't need your routines and compulsions.
We want the old freedom and joy that all things have but you,
Poor white man of the unhappy race.

Corroboree

Hot day dies, cook time comes.
Now between the sunset and the sleep-time
Time of playabout.
The hunters paint black bodies by firelight with designs of meaning
To dance corroboree.
Now didgeridoo compels with haunting drone eager feet to stamp,
Click-sticks click in rhythm to swaying bodies
Dancing corroboree.
Like spirit things in from the great surrounding dark
Ghost-gums dimly seen stand at the edge of light
Watching corroboree.
Eerie the scene in leaping firelight,
Eerie the sounds in that wild setting,
As naked dancers weave stories of the tribe
Into corroboree.

Stone Age

White man, only time is between us.
Once in the time long gone you lived in caves,
You used stone axe, you clothed yourself in skins,
You too feared the dark, fled the unknown.
Go back, remember your own Alcheringa
When lightning still was magic and you hid
From terrible thunder rolling in the sky.
White superior race, only time is between us –
As some are grown up and others yet children.
We are the last of the Stone Age tribes,
Waiting for time to help us
As time helped you.

Assimilation – No!

Pour your pitcher of wine into the wide river
And where is your wine? There is only the river.
Must the genius of an old race die
That the race might live?
We who would be one with you, one people,
We must surrender now much that we love,
The old freedoms for new musts,
Your world for ours,
But a core is left that we must keep always.
Change and compel, slash us into shape,
But not our roots deep in the soil of old.
We are different hearts and minds
In a different body. Do not ask of us
To be deserters, to disown our mother,
To change the unchangeable.
The gum cannot be trained into an oak.
Something is gone, something surrendered, still
We will go forward and learn.
Not swamped and lost, watered away, but keeping
Our own identity, our price of race.
Pour your pitcher of wine into the wide river
And where is your wine? There is only the river.

Integration – Yes!

Gratefully we learn from you,
The advanced race,
You with long centuries of lore behind you.
We who were Australians long before
You who came yesterday,
Eagerly we must learn to change,
Learn new needs we never wanted,
New compulsions never needed,
The price of survival.
Much that we loved is gone and had to go,
But not the deep indigenous things.
The past is still so much a part of us,
Still about us, still within us.
We are happiest
Among our own people. We would like to see
Our own customs kept, our old
Dances and songs, crafts and corroborees.
Why change our sacred myths for your sacred myths?
No, not assimilation but integration,
Not submergence but our uplifting,
So black and white may go forward together
In harmony and brotherhood.

The Teachers

For Mother, who was never
taught to read or write

Holy men, you came to preach:
'Poor black heathen, we will teach
Sense of sin and fear of hell,
Fear of God and boss as well;
We will teach you work for play,
We will teach you to obey
Laws of God and laws of Mammon ...'
And we answered, 'No more gammon,
If you have to teach the light,
Teach us first to read and write.'

Ballad of Totems

My father was Noonuccal man and kept old tribal way,
His totem was the Carpet Snake, whom none must every slay;
But mother was of Peewee clan, and loudly she expressed
The daring view that carpet snakes were nothing but a pest.

Now one lived right inside with us in full immunity,
For no one dared to interfere with father's stern decree:
A mighty fellow ten feet long, and as we lay in bed
We kids could watch him round a beam not far above our head.

Only the dog was scared of him, we'd hear its whines and growls,
But mother fiercely hated him because he took her fowls.
You should have heard her diatribes that flowed in angry torrents
With words you never see in print, except in D. H. Lawrence.

'I kill that robber,' she would scream, fierce as a spotted cat;
'You see that bulge inside him? My speckly hen made that!'
But father's loud and strict command made even mother quake;
I think he'd sooner kill a man than a carpet snake.

That reptile was a greedy-guts, and as each bulge digested
He'd come down on the hunt at night as appetite suggested.
We heard his stealthy slithering sound across the earthen floor,
While the dog gave a startled yelp and bolted out the door.

Then over in the chicken-yard hysterical fowls gave tongue,
Loud frantic squawks accompanied by the barking of the mung,
Until at last the racket passed, and then to solve the riddle,
Next morning he was back up there with a new bulge in his middle.

When father died and we wailed and cried, our grief was deep and sore;
And strange to say from that sad day the snake was seen no more.
The wise old men explained to us: 'It was his tribal brother,
And that is why it done a guy' – but some looked hard at mother.

She seemed to have a secret smile, her eyes were smug and wary,
She looked as innocent as the cat that ate the pet canary.
We never knew, but anyhow (to end this tragic rhyme)
I think we all had snake for tea one day about that time.

White Man, Dark Man

WHITE MAN

Abo man, we
To you have brought
Our social science,
And you we have taught
Our white democracy.

DARK MAN

White man, who
Would teach us and tame,
We had socialism
Long before you came,
And democracy too.

WHITE MAN

Poor blackfellow,
All you ever had
Was ancestor Biami,
Except the big bad
Bunyip and his bellow!

DARK MAN

White fellow, true
You had more for pride:
You had Jesus Christ,
But Him you crucified,
And still do.

The Protectors

While many despise and would exploit us
There are good white men will help us,
But not the appointed and paid officials,
Not the feudal police Protectors,
The protectors who do not protect.

The police of the little far inland towns,
The Protectors of Aborigines
Who move us about at will like cattle
At the request of graziers and their wives:
We feel like owned animals of the Sergeant,
The protector who does not protect.

Is there rape of dark girl by white man or men?
There is no question even of inquiry;
There is no remedy, there is no appeal.
Whom can we appeal to but the Protector
Who feels only contempt for the blacks?
The feeling is mutual, Sergeant!

He sees dark children left without schooling,
Women working from dawn to dark, trapped and unhappy;
He jokes with the rest about storekeepers robbing the blacks,
He is content with all this,
The little local overlord with all power over us,
The protector who does not protect.

Intolerance

White the white glug contemptuously
Says 'nigger', it is plain to me
He is of lower grade than we.

When the dark stockman, used to hate,
Is note accepted as a mate,
Democracy is empty prate.

When we hear from the white élite
'We won't have abos in our street,'
Their Christianity's a cheat.

When blacks are banned, as we know well,
From city café and hotel,
The stink of Little Rock we smell.

Dark children coming home in tears,
Hurt and bewildered by their jeers –
I think Christ weeps with you, my dears.

People who say, by bias driven,
That colour must not be forgiven,
Would snub the Carpenter in heaven.

Bwalla the Hunter

In the hard famine time, in the long drought
Bwalla the hunter on walkabout,
Lubra and children following slow,
All proper hungry long time now.

No more kangaroo out on the plain,
Gone to other country where there was rain.
Couldn't find emu, couldn't find seed,
And the children all time cry for feed.

They saw great eagle come through the sky
To his big stick gunya in a gum near by,
Fine young wallaby carried in his feet:
He bring tucker for his kids to eat.

Big fella eagle circled slow,
Little fella eagles fed below.
'Gwa!' said Bwalla the hunter, 'he
Best fella hunter, better than me.'

He dropped his boomerang. 'Now I climb,
All share tucker in the hungry time.
We got younks too, we got need –
You make fire and we all have feed.'

Then up went Bwalla like a native cat,
All the blackfellows climb like that.
And when he look over big nest rim
Those young ones all sing out at him.

They flapped and spat, they snapped and clawed,
They plenty wild with him, my word,
They shrilled at tucker-thief big and brown,
But Bwalla took wallaby and then climbed done.

No More Boomerang

No more boomerang
No more spear;
Now all civilised –
Colour bar and beer.

No more corroboree,
Gay dance and din.
Now we got movies,
And pay to go in.

No more sharing
What the hunter brings.
Now we work for money,
Then pay it back for things.

Now we track bosses
To catch a few bob,
Now we go walkabout
On bus to the job.

One time naked,
Who never knew shame;
Now we put clothes on
To hide whatsaname.

No more gunya,
Now bungalow,

Paid by hire purchase
In twenty year or so.

Lay down the stone axe,
Take up the steel,
And work like a nigger
For a white man meal.

No more firesticks
That made the whites scoff.
Now all electric
And no better off.

Bunyip he finish,
Now got instead
White fell Bunyip,
Call him Red.

Abstract picture now –
What they coming at?
Cripes, in our caves we
Did better than that.

Black hunted wallaby,
White hunt dollar;
White fella witch-doctor
Wear dog-collar.

No more message-stick;
Lubras and lads
Got television now,
Mostly ads.

Lay down the woomera,
Lay down the waddy.
Now we got atom-bomb,
End *every*body.

Bora

Stone Age youth
Impatient for the testing
Waits command of elders
To face Bora ordeal.
Boyhood is over,
No more now
Playing with the children,
Keeping with the women;
Today at the Bora
Terrified but eager
Boy becomes man.

He will not dare
To cry when the stone knife
Shapes bleeding Bora marks
Of manhood and honour.
Deep scorn and anger
Should he fail the man test.

He will be given now
Woomera and firesticks,
Given balanced boomerang,
War shield and spear.
He will be tracker now
A tribesman, a fighter,
Sitting with the men now,
Dancing in corroboree;

Going with the hunters
To prove himself a man.

Proudly he'll return now
From his first stalking,
Flinging down his weapons,
Flinging down the kill.
The children he played with
See a boy no longer,
He who passed the Bora,
He who bears a man's marks,
He who knows what men know,
All the tribal secrets.

Now as man Bora-made
He has right to lubra.
With eyes shy and shining
She whom he is given
Peeps through her fingers:
This is her man.
Glad she will follow him,
Wait upon her man's word,
Care for his every need,
In their own gunya
Proud to be his woman,
Proud of her man.

Nona

At the happy chattering evening meal
Nona the lithe and lovely,
Liked by all,
Came out of her mother's gunya,
Naked like the rest, and like the rest
Unconscious of her body
As the dingo pup rolling about in play.
All eyes turned, men and women, all
Had smiles for Nona.
And what did the women see? They saw
The white head-band above her forehead,
The gay little feather-tuft in her hair
Fixed with gum, and how she wore it.
They saw the necklet of red berries
And the plaited and painted reed arm-band
Jarri had made her.
And what did the men see? Ah, the men.
They did not see armlet or band
Or the bright little feather-tuft in her hair.
They had no eye for the red berries,
They did no look at these things at all.

The Food Gatherers

We are the food gatherers, we
And all the busy lives we see,
Fur and feathers, the large and small,
With Nature's plenty for us all:
The hawk circling over the plains,
The dingo, scourge of his domains,
The lone owl who voice forlorn
Pursues the sunset into dawn.
Even the small bronze chickowee
That gossips in bright melody –
Look, into the clump he's gone,
He has a little murder on!
For food is life and life is still
The old carnage, and all must kill
Others, though why wise Nature planned
Red rapine, who can understand?
Only for food, never for sport,
That new evil the white man brought.
Lovely to see them day to day,
The food gatherers, busy and gay,
But most of all we love our own,
When as the dulled red sun goes down
Fishers and hunters home return
To where the family fires burn.
Food now and merriment,
Bellies fill and all content,
Around the fires at wide nightfall,
This is the happiest time of all.

Aboriginal Charter of Rights

We want hope, not racialism,
Brotherhood, not ostracism,
Black advance, not white ascendance:
Make us equals, not dependents.
We need help, not exploitation,
We want freedom, not frustration;
Not control, but self-reliance,
Independence, not compliance,
Not rebuff, but education,
Self-respect, not resignation.
Free us from a mean subjection,
From a bureaucrat Protection.
Let's forget the old-time slavers:
Give us fellowship, not favours;
Encouragement, not prohibitions,
Homes, not settlements and missions.
We need love, not overlordship,
Grip of hand, no whip-hand wardship;
Opportunity that places
White and black on equal basis.
You dishearten, not defend us,
Circumscribe, who should befriend us.
Give us welcome, not aversion,
Give us choice, not cold coercion,
Status, not discrimination,
Human rights, not segregation.
You the law, like Roman Pontius,

Make us proud, not colour-conscious;
Give the deal you still deny us,
Give goodwill, not bigot bias;
Give ambition, not prevention,
Confidence, not condescension;
Give incentive, not restriction,
Give us Christ, not crucifixion.
Though baptised and blessed and Bibled
We are still tabooed and libelled.
You devout Salvation-sellers,
Make us neighbours, not fringe-dwellers;
Make us mates, not poor relations,
Citizens, not serfs on stations.
Must we native Old Australians
In our land rank as aliens?
Banish bans and conquer caste,
Then we'll win our own at last.

Note: This poem was prepared and presented to the 5th Annual General Meeting of the Federal Council for the Advancement of Aborigines and Torres Strait Islanders, held in Adelaide, Easter 1962.

Gifts

'I will bring you love', said the young lover,
'A glad light to dance in your dark eye.
Pendants I will bring of the white bone,
And gay parrot feathers to deck your hair.'

But she only shook her head.

'I will put a child in your arms,' he said,
'Will be a great headman, great rain-maker.
I will make remembered songs about you
That all the tribes in all the wandering camps
Will sing for ever.'

But she was not impressed.

'I will bring you the still moonlight on the lagoon,
And steal for you the singing of all the birds;
I will bring down the stars of heaven to you,
And put the bright rainbow into your hand.'

'No,' she said, 'bring me tree-grubs.'

Spinners

Racism:
Destroy it?
How?
The monster
lives
because
It was created
Strong
With white iron will.
Created
To control
Black.
White monster
Uncontrolled
Controls
The maker.
Soon the monster maker
Will die.
A black black monster
With black iron will
Will live
And become master.
Created for the purpose
Of spinning
Wheels
    in wheels
        in wheels.

A Song of Hope

Look up, my people,
The dawn is breaking,
The world is waking
    To a new bright day,
When none defame us,
No restriction tame us,
Nor colour shame us,
    Nor sneer dismay.

Now brood no more
On the years behind you,
The hope assigned you
    Shall the past replace,
When a juster justice
Grown wise and stronger
Points the bone no longer
    At a darker race.

So long we waited
Bound and frustrated,
Till hate be hated
    And caste deposed;
Now light shall guide us,
No goal denied us,
And all doors open
    That long were closed.

See plain the promise,
Dark freedom-lover!
Night's nearly over,
    And though long the climb,
New rights will greet us,
New mateship meet us,
And joy complete us
    In our new Dream Time.

To our fathers' fathers
    The pain, the sorrow;
To our children's children
    The glad tomorrow.

The Woor Woman

Bhoori the hunter left the hill,
For now the western sky was red,
And all the world grew sad and still.

The trees whispered as he went by.
It was a lonely place. He heard
The crake cry and the plover cry.

He stopped and stared. There in the green
A strange woman stood watching him,
The loveliest he had ever seen.

She turned and ran a little way,
Then waited, looking back at him.
'Follow, follow,' she seemed to say.

'Oh, I must follow her,' said he.
'She will be in my dreams for ever
If I let her go from me.'

Again she ran, again she stayed,
And ever led and lured him on
Half eagerly and half afraid,

Until a water barred the way,
The hushed swamp of the Woor Woman
Where none would venture night or day.

Beyond, he saw the water gleam.
'Follow, follow,' she seemed to say.
Bhoori followed as one in dream.

Then out upon the water dim
Lightly she ran and there stood,
Stood on the water watching him.

'Now I have seen it, now I know
She is of the Shadow People.'

And when like friendly comfort came
The red camp fires of his tribe
They welcomed him and called his name.

But Bhoori seemed as one in thrall,
For these to him were now strangers,
Faces he did not know at all.

They heard his tale all wonder-eyed,
And some smiled, but the old men
Shook their heads and talked aside.

'It is the sign of old,' they said
'Bhoori has seen the Woor Woman,
In three days' time we'll find him dead.'

The Dawn Is at Hand

Dark brothers, first Australian race,
Soon you will take your rightful place
In the brotherhood long waited for,
   Fringe-dwellers no more.

Sore, sore the tears you shed
When hope seemed folly and justice dead.
Was the long night weary? Look up, dark band,
   The dawn is at hand.

Go forward proudly and unafraid
To your birthright all too long delayed,
For soon now the shame of the past
   Will be over at last.

You will be welcomed mateship-wise
In industry and in enterprise;
No profession will bar the door,
   Fringe-dwellers no more.

Dark and white upon common ground
In club and office and social round,
Yours the feel of a friendly land,
   The grip of the hand.

Sharing the same equality
In college and university,

All ambitions of hand or brain,
　　Yours to attain

For ban and bias will soon be gone,
The future beckons you bravely on
To art and letters and nation lore,
　　Fringe-dwellers no more.

Municipal Gum

Gumtree in the city street,
Hard bitumen around your feet,
Rather you should be
In the cool world of leafy forest halls
And wild bird calls.
Here you seem to me
Like that poor cart-horse
Castrated, broken, a thing wronged,
Strapped and buckled, its hell prolonged,
Whose hung head and listless mien express
Its hopelessness.
Municipal gum, it is dolorous
To see you thus
Set in your black grass of bitumen –
O fellow citizen,
What have they done to us?

My Love

Possess me? No, I cannot give
    The love that others know,
For I am wedded to a cause:
    The rest I must forgo.

You claim me as your very own,
    My body, soul and mind;
My love is my own people first,
    And after that, mankind.

The social part, the personal
    I have renounced of old;
Mine is dedicated to life,
    No man's to have and hold.

Old white intolerance hems me round,
    Insult and scorn assail;
I must be free, I must be strong
    To fight and not to fail.

For there are ancient wrongs to right,
    Men's malice to endure;
A long road and a lonely road,
    But oh, the goal is sure.

Colour Bar

When vile men jeer because my skin is brown,
This I live down.

But when a taunted child comes home in tears,
Fierce anger sears.

The colour bar! It shows the meaner mind
Of moron kind.

Men are but medieval yet, as long
As lives this wrong.

Could he but see, the colour-baiting clod
Is blaming God

Who made us all, and all His children He
Loves equally.

As long as brothers banned from brotherhood
You still exclude,

The Christianity you hold so high
Is but a lie,

Justice a cant of hypocrites, content
With precedent.

Tribal Justice

Gone the gay laughter of the old happy days,
And all because of Boola and his arrogant ways,
Who broke the good camp code that each tribe obeys.

Leader in the skill games with boomerang and spear,
Ever ready with a scowl, ready with a jeer,
Boola loved to dominate, loved to domineer.

For Boola the masterful scorned the old and wise
With his truculent questions and truculent replies;
Even the wise headman he dared to criticise.

He took married lubras and there was nothing said,
For he was quick to give a blow, he was held in dread.
They feared the wife-stealer so they beat the wives instead.

When the great drought continued they knew what caused the ill:
Some wizard of a far tribe working his evil will,
And they must send a death-band to seek him out and kill.

They called a men's council, but he did not obey.
'Old men all yabba-yabba.' For Boola every day
Was scornful of the elders, and went his own way.

Out at the council talk-place the conference began
To settle who was guilty and make the vengeance plan.
'It could be that Boola,' growled Darg the witch-man.

Then quick eyes met other eyes, and each knew
The thinking of his neighbour, and the silence grew.
'The fellow plenty bad,' agreed an old pinnaroo.

The grey headman spoke to them: 'Gather close about,
We will hold the spirit rites, we will find out.
Let Darg do his magic to see who made the drought.'

They pressed close to watch it, absorbed by the spell
Of the witch-doctor's magic, but now they knew well
How dark omens would be read and what the signs would tell.

When suddenly the fierce band burst on the camp near by
The women screamed, the dogs fled as spears began to fly,
And frantic Boola saw too late he was the one to die.

A camp moves when death comes, and they made haste to go,
No wailing for dead Boola, no tree-grave would he know;
They left him on the ground there for carrion kite and crow.

Artist Son

To Kabul of the tribe Noonuccal (Vivian Walker)

My artist son,
Busy with brush, absorbed in more than play,
Untutored yet, striving alone to find
What colour and form can say,
Yours the deep human need,
The old compulsion, ever since man had mind
And learned to dream,
Adventuring, creative, unconfined.
Even in dim beginning days,
Long before written word was known,
Your fathers too fashioned their art
Who had but bark and wood and the cave stone.
Much you must learn from others, yes,
But copy none; follow no fashions, know
Art the adventurer his lone way
Lonely must go.
Paint joy, not pain.
Paint beauty and happiness for men,
Paint the rare insight glimpses that express
What tongue cannot or pen;
Not for reward, acclaim
That wins honour and opens doors,
Not as ambition toils for fame,
But as the lark sings and the eagle soars.
Make us songs in colour and line:
Painting is speech, painter and poet are one.
Paint what you feel more than the thing you see,
My artist son.

Son of Mine
(To Denis)

My son, your troubled eyes search mine,
Puzzled and hurt by colour line.
Your black skin soft as velvet shine;
What can I tell you, son of mine?

I could tell you of heartbreak, hatred blind,
I could tell of crimes that shame mankind,
Of brutal wrong and deeds malign,
Of rape and murder, son of mine;

But I'll tell instead of brave and fine
When lives of black and white entwine,
And men in brotherhood combine –
This would I tell you, son of mine.

Dead Life

I dare not live too long
Life may last for ever.
In a span of life
Ten million lives are lost
And few are found.

Dead men roam
The streets
Screaming obscenities,
Cursing, damning.
Forcing me to look
At my dead life
And theirs.

?

Hello tree;
Talk to me.
I'm sick
And lonely.

Are you old?
Trunk so cold.
What secrets
Do you hold?

Talk tree!
Can't you see;
My troubles
Trouble me.

Silent tree
Let me see
Your answers.
ANSWER ME.

Tree!
You dare
Question ME?
How dare you
Dare, question ME.

Jarri's Love Song

Outside his new-made gunya Jarri
With a sudden howl started to make a song.
He had something to sing about, he
Had been given the pretty Nona,
He was making a song about Nona.
Jarri never made song to remember
But many times he made camp laugh.
Now they laughed at Jarri's love song,
They all liked that cheerful fellow, all
But sour old Yundi.
Jarri sat with legs out
Thudding a hollow log with waddy
To make rhythm, he raised voice
To the yelling chant of the good song-men
Nona laughed with them, proud of Jarri,
Happy to share all eyes with Jarri.
Only old Yundi scowled.
And this the love song Jarri sang them:

I got belly-bruise from a club,
But I ... got ... Nona!
I got a sore where I sit down
But I ... got ... Nona.
Lost 'em firesticks, broke it woomera,
No more fishnet, no more tomahawk,
Got no gooreen, got no shield,
But I ... got ... Nona.

Gootchi he got bark canoe
But I ... got ... Nona.
Yarrawan sleep with hunting-dog
But I got Nona.
Kaa got pitcheri, Gwabba got drone-pipe,
Mullawa he got three boomerangs and two dingoes,
Walla got possum-rug keep him warm,
But I ... got ... Nona.

Gecko fella, he got two tails,
But I ... got ... Nona.
Frog he only got other frog
But I ... got ... Nona.
Gwoon got Weela with big hind part,
She got seven kids before he start,
Grey old Yundi got withered old Yan,
But I ... got ... Nona.

Note: Gooreen, a heavy throwing-stick used in hunting. Pitcheri (pituri), a native plant gathered and chewed by some tribes for its narcotic properties. The little gecko lizard seen on tree trunks easily sheds its tail when seized, and this often saves its life. The tail grows again but the new growth is often abnormal, and geckoes with double tails are to be seen.

Community Rain Song

At the old tribal squatting-place
Behind the camp gunyas
Tonight they were doing their Wyambi rain song
Under the bright stars.
This was nardoo-gathering season
But now little nardoo. Too long dry,
Grass all brown, birds not breeding,
Creeks not running, clouds gone long time.
This not a ritual secret and sacred,
This a camp game, a community playabout,
Even the women there, even the children.
But some of the old men, aloof and grave
Throughout all the laughter muttered strange words
Of magic-making as old as the race,
Handed down through countless generations,
Not understood now but faithfully repeated,
Lost rain-words from ancestral times.
Behind the bushes sounded
The weird whirring drone of the dread bullroarer,
While all waited motionless
As a great figure-group carved in stone
Dim in the firelight.

Now into view with dance steps advancing
A line of painted song-men
Chanting in unison:
'Rain come down!
Rain come down!'
And the squatting horde in chorus:

'Rain come down!'
'Creek run soon!
Creek run soon!
You great sky ones, fill dry waterhole,
Send rain down!'
'Creek run soon!
Send rain down!'

'Rainbird come,
That fellow know, he talk and tell us
Rain fall down!'
At once the whole Wyambi people
Took up the loud toneless scream
Of the giant cuckoo they called the rainbird

Whose coming always predicted rain.
A rhythm of 'Rain fall down!' mingled
With the harsh calls of the bird.

'Frog talk now,
Wake up now,
Frog fellow singing out, they telling all about
Rain come down!'
Joyously then the tribe came in
With the croaking of frogs little and big,
Filling a swamp with bedlam of joy
At the nearness of rain:
'Wark, awark, wark!'
'Eek, eek, cree-eek!'
'Ork! Ork!'

'Plover here now,
Plover loud now,
He sure rain-bringer, he tell blackfellow
Rain fall down!'
From all the rows of people now
Came perfectly the spurwinged plover's sharp
Excited staccato:
'Karra-karak!'
'Keerk-keerk!'
'Karaka-karra-karak!'

'Wind he come,
Little wind first time,
He say soon big blow follow him
And rain fall down!'
'Wee-oo, Whoo-oo!' came the wail of the wind,
'Whish-awhee-ee!'
'Awhoo-whoo!'

'Thunder up there,
Rumble up there,
Dooloomai the Thunderer he tumble all about,
Shake rain down!'
Like answer came a deep rolling thunder
From the men, while the women with open palms
Beat rapidly upon skin rugs

Stretched taut between their knees like drums
Till the hollow sound

Swelled to a loud booming and then
Gradually died away.

'Rain come down! Rain come down!'
Chorused the line of dancers, threw
Into the air handfuls of water
From bark yorlis as they stamped and swayed,
Chanting
The repetitions of the rain song,
While from the ranked Wyambis rose
The toneless monotone of showers,
Hard to do and done superbly –
Leafy boughs, rattling gravel, voices, all
Blended as one to reproduce
The universal sound of steady rain.
The tempo increased, all the rain symbols now
Mingled in pandemonium. Frogs croaked,
Rainbird screamed, thunder rolled,
The rising whine of wind
Cut across cries of plover, and
As background to it all
The deep steady drumming of the rain:
'Wark, awark-wark!'
'Wee-whoo-awhoo!'
'Karra-karak-karak! '
'Boom! Bombomba-oom-m-m!'
'Cree-eek! Ork! Ork!'
'Whish-awhee-ee!'

'Rain come down! Rain come down!'
It looked like going on half the night.
A dingo on a low ridge
Half a mile away
Stood motionless with pricked ears looking down
On the strange goings-on below, dim-lit
By the dying Wyambi fires. These
Were the feared and hated men-creatures
Nothing in all the bush could understand.
He turned away into the dark.

Down on the squatting-place,
Lost in the merry-making, no one marked
The rising of a little wind
That rustled the belahs and then began
To sway them; none saw
That the clear stars above them had disappeared.

Suddenly
A blinding white fork of lightning
Stood for an instant close above them
And instantaneously
A double shattering crash of thunder
That shook the world. All sprang up
Laughing and screaming,
Half in terror and half in joy as the first
Slow drops of rain began to fall; the wind
Whipped up to a gale and whooped about them,
Sparks from the fires

Went whirled in showers across the dark
As the rain roared to a downpour.
'The caves! The caves!'
Some snatched up firesticks and in a straggling line
The excited Wyambi people
Went streaming off along the empty creek
Towards the great red caves of sandstone where
They sheltered at night in the worst wet weather.
Oi! Oi! Good playabout that time!
Oi! Oi! A night to be remembered.

Namatjira

Aboriginal man, you walked with pride,
And painted with joy the countryside.
Original man, your fame grew fast,
Men pointed you out as you went past.

But vain the honour and tributes paid,
For you strangled in rules the white men made;
You broke no law of your own wild clan
Which says, 'Share all with your fellow-man.'

What did their loud acclaim avail
Who gave you honour, then gave you jail?
Namatjira, they boomed your art,
They called you genius, then broke your heart.

The Dispossessed

For Uncle Willie Mackenzie

Peace was yours, Australian man, with tribal laws you made,
Till white Colonials stole your peace with rape and murder raid;
They shot and poisoned and enslaved until, a scattered few,
Only a remnant now remain, and the heart dies in you.
The white man claimed your hunting grounds and you could not remain,
They made you work as menials for greedy private gain;
Your tribes are broken vagrants now wherever whites abide,
And justice of the white man means justice to you denied.
They brought you Bibles and disease, the liquor and the gun:
With Christian culture such as these the white command was won.
A dying race you linger on, degraded and oppressed,
Outcasts in your own native land, you are the dispossessed.

When Churches mean a way of life, as Christians proudly claim,
And when hypocrisy is scorned and hate is counted shame,
Then only shall intolerance die and old injustice cease,
And white and dark as brothers find equality and peace.
But oh, so long the wait has been, so slow the justice due,
Courage decays for want of hope, and the heart dies in you.

Interlude

Their conversation arrested me. There I was, turned off, relaxing on a garden chair, watching early night swallow the last of the daylight.

In the dusk, two forms came into focus. One was shaking his head and his long hair and beard were outlined against the fading light. He was wearing a long gown. He was telling the other shade where he came from. The other shadow had a beard too. They both looked like socially deprived dropouts. One even poorer than the other. He was naked.

Their skins were dark like they must have got an over-exposure of sun. One was dark dark and the other sort of not-so-dark dark.

The not-so-dark darkie was talking and using his hands to make a point. The other dark darkie noticed the holes in the palms of his hands and asked him, how come.

The not-so-dark darkie dropped his hands and frowned, as though he wasn't sure he should tell the dark darkie his story.

He mentioned something about a cause and a betrayal, but as it happened so long ago he'd just sooner forget it.

The dark darkie said he thought nailing people to bits of wood a bit too crude for him. In his neck of the wood, they killed a man quick and clean. Torture like that wasn't their cup of tea.

The not-so-dark darkie said he didn't hold any grudge in spite of what they had done. The dark darkie said he sounded like a hippie-crit. If his gang had of done that to him, he would have returned in spirit form and put the fear of christ into them all.

The not-so-dark darkie replied he didn't have to, they did just that to themselves. He often heard them saying things like for christ sake, or christ almighty, etcetera, etcetera.

Then he explained to the dark darkie that after they had tortured him to death, they renamed him. Dark darkie asks why. He replied christ knows, that was what sent the cult haywire in the first place.

Everyone wanted to get in on the act. Each generation trying to outsmart the last. Trying to build a bigger and bigger hippiecritter outsmart the last. Trying to build a bigger and bigger hippiecritter movement. The greedy ones finally got the power away from the others and they used his image as a morale booster and bogey man. Sometimes he was even called the hero of the movement. Then he went on to explain the counter revolutionists within the movement. All races setting up their own particular brand of the movement and trying to run the show.

During the breakaway, they decided to rename him. Now the movement was in such a hell of a mess, he regretted ever starting it. Now togetherness is obsolete as far as they are concerned.

The dark darkie said he felt sorry for him. He sure was a troubled soul. He was glad he did not have that on his plate. Probably because he didn't complicate matters in the first place like the not-so-dark darkie had done. He explained his job was offsiding to a female serpent and he and his gang had the job of spreading peace and love around. He admitted he too had trouble getting his scattered gangs together again, since the Christian invaders had come and torn the guts out of them.

The not-so-dark darkie explained he had ideas of peace and love too. Every time they slapped him he turned the other cheek and before he knew it they had him nailed.

The dark darkie shakes his head, looks up at the rain clouds above and says he's overspent his time and that he'd better get back to shadow land before closing. Said he'd enjoyed talking to a hippie-critter.

The not-so-dark darkie lifts up his holey hands and says, same here, and to hell with them all, he'd let them carry their own crosses from now on. He was becoming allergic to crosses.

Suddenly a clap of thunder and down came the rain. The two shadows hit the dust and I ran up the stairs, into the light.

The Bunyip

You keep quiet now, little fella,
You want big-big Bunyip get you?
You look out, no good this place.
You see that waterhole over there?
He Gooboora, Silent Pool.
Suppose-it you go close up one time
Big fella woor, he wait there,
Big fella Bunyip sit down there,
In Silent Pool many bones down there.
He come up when it is dark,
He belong the big dark, that one.
Don't go away from camp fire, you,
Better you curl up in the gunya,
Go to sleep now, little fella,
Tonight he hungry, hear him roar,
He frighten us, the terrible woor,
He the secret thing, he Fear,
He something we don't know.
Go to sleep now, little fella,
Curl up with the yella dingo.

Understand, Old One

Understand, old one,
I mean no desecration
Staring here with the learned ones
At your opened grave.
Now after hundreds of years gone
The men of science coming with spade and knowledge
Peer and probe, handle the yellow bones,
To them specimens, to me
More. Deeply moved am I.

Understand, old one,
I mean no lack of reverence.
It is with love
I think of you so long ago laid here
With tears and wailing.
Strongly I feel your presence very near
Haunting the old spot, watching
As we disturb your bones. Poor ghost,
I know, I know you will understand.

What if you came back now
To our new world, the city roaring
There on the old peaceful camping place
Of your red fires along the quiet water,
How you would wonder
At towering stone gunyas high in air
Immense, incredible;

Planes in the sky over, swarms of cars
Like things frantic in flight.
What if you came at night upon these miles
Of clustered neon lights of all colours
Like Christian newly come to his Heaven or Hell
And your own people gone?
Old one of the long ago,
So many generations lie between us
But cannot estrange. Your duty to your race
Was with the simple past, mine
Lies in the present and the coming days.

Note: This came after I had visited an old native burial ground not far from Brisbane, where University people were excavating bones and had invited me along. I wrote it down at once while impressions were still fresh.

Gooboora, the Silent Pool

For Grannie Sunflower, Last of the Noonuccals

Gooboora, Gooboora, the Water of Fear
That awed the Noonuccals once numerous here,
The Bunyip is gone from your bone-strewn bed,
And the clans departed to drift with the dead.

Once in the far time before the whites came
How light were their hearts in the dance and the game!
Gooboora, Gooboora, to think that today
A whole happy tribe are all vanished away!

What mystery lurks by the Water of Fear,
And what is the secret still lingering here?
For birds hasten by as in days of old,
No wild thing will drink of your waters cold.

Gooboora, Gooboora, still here you remain,
But where are my people I look for in vain?
They are gone from the hill, they are gone from the shore,
And the place of the Silent Pool knows them no more.

But I think they still gather when daylight is done
And stand round the pool at the setting of sun,
A shadowy band that is now without care,
Fearing no longer the Thing in its lair.

Old Death has passed by you but took the dark throng;
Now lost is the Noonuccal language and song.
Gooboora, Gooboora, it makes the heart sore
That you should be here but my people no more!

We Are Going

For Grannie Coolwell

They came into the little town
A semi-naked band subdued and silent,
All that remained of their tribe.
They came here to the place of their old bora ground
Where now the many white men hurry about like ants.
Notice of estate agents reads: 'Rubbish May Be Tipped Here.'
Now it half covers the traces of the old bora ring.
They sit and are confused, they cannot say their thoughts:
'We are as strangers here now, but the white tribe are the strangers.
We belong here, we are of the old ways.
We are the corroboree and the bora ground,
We are the old sacred ceremonies, the laws of the elders.
We are the wonder tales of Dream Time, the tribal legends told.
We are the past, the hunts and the laughing games, the wandering
    camp fires.
We are the lightning-bolt over Gaphembah Hill
Quick and terrible,
And the Thunder after him, that loud fellow.
We are the quiet daybreak paling the dark lagoon.
We are the shadow-ghosts creeping back as the camp fires burn low.
We are nature and the past, all the old ways
Gone now and scattered.
The scrubs are gone, the hunting and the laughter.
The eagle is gone, the emu and the kangaroo are gone from this place.
The bora ring is gone.
The corroboree is gone.
And we are going.'

Cookalingee

For Elsie Lewis

Cookalingee, now all day
Station cook in white man's way,
Dressed and fed, provided for,
Sees outside her kitchen door
Ragged band of her own race,
Hungry nomads, black of face.
Never begging, they stand by,
Silent, waiting, wild and shy,
For they know that in their need
Cookalingee gives them feed.
Peeping in, their deep dark eyes
Stare at stove with wide surprise,
Pots and pans and kitchen-ware,
All the white-man wonders there.

Cookalingee, lubra still
Spite of white-man station drill,
Knows the tribal laws of old:
'Share with others what you hold;'
Hears the age-old racial call:
'What we have belongs to all.'
Now she gives with generous hand
White man tucker to that band,
Full tin plate and pannikin
To each hunter, child and gin.
Joyful, on the ground they sit,
With only hands for eating it.

Then upon their way they fare,
Bellies full and no more care.

Cookalingee, lubra still
Feels her dark eyes softly fill,
Watching as they go content,
Natural as nature meant.
And for all her place and pay
Is she happy now as they?

Wistfully she muses on
Something bartered, something gone.
Songs of old remembered days,
The walkabout, the old free ways.
Blessed with everything she prized,
Trained and safe and civilised,
Much she has that they have not,
But is hers the happier lot?

Lonely in her paradise
Cookalingee sits and cries.

United We Win

The glare of a thousand years is shed on the black man's wistful face,
Fringe-dweller now on the edge of towns, one of a dying race;
But he has no bitterness in his heart for the white man just the same;
He knows he has white friends today, he knows they are not to blame.
Curse no more the nation's great, the glorious pioneers,
Murderers honoured with fame and wealth, won of our blood and tears;
Brood no more on the bloody past that is gone without regret,
But look to the light of happier days that will shine for your children yet.
For in spite of public apathy and the segregation pack
There is mateship now, and the good white hand stretched out to grip the black.
He knows there are white friends here today who will help us fight the past,
Till a world of workers from shore to shore as equals live at last.

Song

Life is ours in vain
Lacking love, which never
Counts the loss or gain.
But remember, ever
Love is linked with pain.

Light and sister shade
Shape each mortal morrow
Seek not to evade
Love's companion Sorrow,
And be not dismayed.

Grief is not in vain,
It's for our completeness.
If the fates ordain
Love to bring life sweetness,
Welcome too its pain.

God's One Mistake
(It repenteth me that I have made man. - Genesis, 6)

I who am ignorant and know so little,
So little of life and less of God,
This I do know
That happiness is intended and could be,
That all wild simple things have life fulfilled
Save man,
That all on earth have natural happiness
Save man.
Without books or schools, lore or philosophy
In my own heart I know
That hate is wrong,
Injustice evil.
Pain there must be and tears,
Sorrow and death, but not
Intolerance, unkindness, cruelty,
Unless men choose
The mean and base, which Nature never made,
But we alone.
And sometimes I will think that God looks down
With loving smile, saying,
'Poor child, poor child, maybe I was wrong
In planning for you reason and free will
To fashion your own life in your own way.
For all the rest
I settled and appointed as for children
Their simple days, but you
I gave the Godlike gift to choose,
Who were not wise – for see how you have chosen,
Poor child, alone among them all now
Unhappy on the earth.'

Verses

I

After all creeds since reason first began,
Though it seems odd,
I'm still uncertain whether God made man
Or man made God.

II

When someone invented the rope
It wasn't so long till some other
Improved its use by inventing the noose,
And we started to hang one another.

III

Appearance is the world's test.
Brother, you're treated as you're dressed.

IV

'Man born of woman is a mess.
Adam alone was perfect man.'
'Aw, I don't know,' piped little Joe,
'He had no belly-button, Gran.'

V

Of all the ways to waste our days
Whose lives are short at best,
Listening to piano solos
Is one of the dreariest.

VI

'Prate not of God whom none has seen,
Poor dupe as credulous as blind.'
Wiseacre who must see to know,
You've never seen your own behind.

VII

Man's endless quest is to be happy,
Ever since Cain wet his first nappy;
Yet crime-waves now and A-bomb plans,
And Yanks turned Schickelgruber fans.

VIII

If Christ returned today among us, he
Once more would meet cold eye of Sadducee,
Security Boys would whisper and insist,
McCarthyites would chorus 'Communist!'

IX

Don't say Sir Boodle Blimp ignores the arts.
For golf his culture is both deep and strong;
Financial columns are his poetry;
His favourite music is the dinner gong.

X

All our lives my brothers, we
Have fought for a just equality.
Patience! At last it will be found:
We are all equal under the ground.

Civilisation

We who came late to civilisation,
Missing a gap of centuries,
When you came we marvelled and admired,
But with foreboding.
We had so little but we had happiness,
Each day a holiday,
For we were people before we were citizens,
Before we were ratepayers,
Tenants, customers, employees, parishioners.
How could we understand
White man's gradings, rigid and unquestioned,
Your sacred totems of Lord and Lady,
Highness and Holiness, Eminence, Majesty.
We could not understand
Your strange cult of uniformity,
This mass obedience to clocks, time-tables.
Puzzled, we wondered why
The importance to you, urgent and essential,
Of ties and gloves, shoe-polish, uniforms.
New to us were jails and orphanages,
Rents and taxes, banks and mortgages.
We who had so few things, the prime things,
We had no policemen, lawyers, middlemen,
Brokers, financiers, millionaires.
So they bewildered us, all the new wonders,
Stocks and shares, real estate,

Compound interest, sales and investments.
Oh, we have benefited, we have been lifted
With new knowledge, a new world opened.
Suddenly caught up in white man's ways
Gladly and gratefully we accept,
For this is necessity.
But remember, white man, if life is for happiness,
You too, surely, have much to change.

Biami

'Mother, what is that one sea,
Sometimes blue or green or yellow?'
'That Biami's waterhole.
He big fellow.'

'Mother, what make sunset fire,
Every night the big red glare?'
'Biami's gunya out that way,
That his camp fire over there.'

'How come great wide river here,
Where we swim and fish with spear?'
'Biami dug him.
You see big hills all about?
They the stuff that he chuck out.'

Note: Among white people Biami is the best known of the great Aboriginal Ancestors who made the world and men. They were not gods, not worshipped, but were highly venerated.

Freedom

For Vivian Charles

Brumby on the wide plain,
All men out to break you,
My warm fellow-feeling
Hopes they never take you!

Dingo on the lone ridge,
Fleeing as you spy them,
Every hand against you,
May you still defy them!

All things wild and tameless,
Hunted down and hated,
Something in my wild heart
With your own is mated.

Dingo, wild bushranger,
Brumby that they ban so,
May you still outmatch them,
May you foil the man-foe!

Return to Nature

Lover of my happy past
Soothe my weariness
With warm embrace.
Turn not from me,
Communicate.
Am I strayed too long
And now forsaken?
Your cold winds freeze
My offered love.

Was it yesterday
Or a thousand years,
My eager feet
Caressed your paths;
My opened fingers
Counted grains of sand
Hidden in the warmth of time.

Now my civilised self
Stamps its imprint
On reluctant sands
And time has flown.
Impatient to converse
My brutalness
Turns you from my touch –
Oh lost, neglected love,
My tear-stained eyes
Open now to see
Your enemy and mine
Is – civilised me.

Hope

As tribal elders sit,
Their tribal thoughts tie their tongue.
We, the foreigners,
In this our land,
Know not
Where lies our future track.
No place forward,
None back.

Hearing their city tribes
Talk the foreign tongue,
They shuffle their tribal feet,
And wait,
And judge,
And soon, within their age-old eyes,
A light appears:
Yes, it was there,
Though but a pinhead size.

Frustrated still
They walk away,
With knowing smile
And gentle voice.
Now ...
We hope ...
For you have taught us
... hope ... there is.

Racism

Stalking the corridors of life,
Black, frustrated minds
Scream for release
From christian racist moulds .
Moulds that enslave
Black independence.

Take care! white racists!
Blacks can be racists too.
A violent struggle could erupt
And racists meet their death.

Colour, the gift of nature
To mankind,
Is now the contentious bone,
And black-white hatred sustains itself
On the rotting, putrid flesh
That once was man.

I Am Proud

I am black of skin among whites,
And I am proud,
Proud of race and proud of skin.
I am broken and poor,
Dressed in rags from white man's back,
But do not think I am ashamed.
Spears could not contend against guns and we were mastered,
But there are things they could not plunder and destroy.
We were conquered but never subservient,
We were compelled but never servile.
Do not think I cringe as white men cringe to whites.
I am proud,
Though humble and poor and without a home ...
So was Christ.

Then and Now

In my dreams I hear my tribe
Laughing as they hunt and swim,
But dreams are shattered by rushing car,
By grinding tram and hissing train,
And I see no more my tribe of old
As I walk alone in the teeming town.

I have seen corroboree
Where that factory belches smoke;
Here where they have memorial park
One time lubras dug for yams;
One time our dark children played
There where the railway yards are now,
And where I remember the didgeridoo
Calling to us to dance and play,
Offices now, neon lights now,
Bank and shop and advertisement now,
Traffic and trade of the busy town.

No more woomera, no more boomerang,
No more playabout, no more the old ways .
Children of nature we were then,
No clocks hurrying crowds to toil.
Now I am civilised and work in the white way,
Now I have dress, now I have shoes:
'Isn't she lucky to have a good job! '
Better when I had only a dillybag.
Better when I had nothing but happiness.

Daisy Bindi

Slavery at Roy Hill, to our shame profound,
Wages for the blacks nil all the year round,
Slavers given free hand by police consent,
Winked at obligingly by Government.
But a woman warrior where aid there was none
Led her dark people till the fight was won.

    Salute to a spirit fine,
    Daisy of Nullagine,
    Who unaided resolutely
    Dared to challenge slavery.

Tall Daisy Bindi, she rode like a man,
Mustering and stockwork from when dawn began,
And long chores indoors that made life bleak
Year after weary year for nothing a week,
Till Daisy of the stout heart organised her clan
To strike for native justice and the plain rights of man.

    High praise and honour to
    Daisy of the Noongahs who
    Fought and routed tyranny,
    Dared to challenge slavery.

Oh, the boss men threatened and the boss men swore,
They called the police in to help break the law,

And dark men and women were forced and assailed,
For fighting degradation they were bashed and jailed,
But Daisy the militant no man subdued,
Who championed her people out of servitude.

Note: Mrs Daisy Bindi of Western Australia's far inland made a name for herself as an Aboriginal leader of her people. On Roy Hill Station where she worked, the native stockmen and domestics received no wages till at last she organised them and fought for the rights of her race. It was a long struggle and marked by disgraceful incidents against the Aboriginals concerned, but the final result was victory and the establishment of the admirable Pindan Co-operative Aboriginal community at Port Hedland.

The Past

Let no one say the past is dead.
The past is all about us and within.
Haunted by tribal memories, I know
This little now, this accidental present
Is not the all of me, whose long making
Is so much of the past.

Tonight here in suburbia as I sit
In easy chair before electric heater,
Warmed by the red glow, I fall into dream:
I am away
At the camp fire in the bush, among
My own people, sitting on the ground,
No walls about me,
The stars over me,
The tall surrounding trees that stir in the wind
Making their own music,
Soft cries of the night coming to us, there
Where we are one with all old Nature's lives
Known and unknown,
In scenes where we belong but have now forsaken.
Deep chair and electric radiator
Are but since yesterday,
But a thousand thousand camp fires in the forest
Are in my blood.
Let none tell me the past is wholly gone.
Now is so small a part of time, so small a part
Of all the race years that have moulded me.

Time Is Running Out

The miner rapes
The heart of earth
With his violent spade.
Stealing, bottling her black blood
For the sake of greedy trade.
On his metal throne of destruction,
He labours away with a will,
Piling the mountainous minerals high
With giant tool and iron drill.

In his greedy lust for power,
He destroys old nature's will.
For the sake of the filthy dollar,
He dirties the nest he builds.
Well he knows that violence
Of his destructive kind
Will be violently written
Upon the sands of time.

But time is running out
And time is close at hand,
For the Dreamtime folk are massing
To defend their timeless land.
Come gentle black man
Show your strength;
Time to take a stand.
Make the violent miner feel
Your violent
Love of land.

Balance

Spin a coin:
Life or death.
Next of kin
To death
Is life,
And life
To death.

Light comes
Before dark.
In life we wait
The birth of death.

China ... Woman

High peaked mountains
Stand out against the skyline.
The great Wall
Twines itself
Around and over them,
Like my Rainbow Serpent,
Groaning her way
Through ancient rocks.
I hear the heavy tramp
Of the liberating army,
Shaking the mountains loose,
Of rolling stones.
Falling, crushing,
The weeping wild flowers
In their path.
China, the woman,
Stands tall,
Breasts heavy
With the milk of her labours,
Pregnant with expectation.
The ancient Dynasties
Sleep.
Emperors are entombed
In museums.

The people of China
Are now the custodians of palaces.
And the wise old
Lotus plants
Nod their heads
In agreement.

Reed Flute Cave

I didn't expect to meet you in Guilin
My Rainbow Serpent,
My Earth Mother,
But you were there
In Reed Flute Cave,
With animals and reptiles
And all those things
You stored in the Dreamtime.
Pools of cool water, like mirrors,
Reflecting your underbelly.

The underground storage place,
Where frogs store water in their stomachs
And mushrooms and every type of fruit,
Vegetable, animal and fish,
Are on display.

Perhaps I have strayed too long
In this beautiful country;
The reed flutes are playing a mournful tune.
The cool air rushing through
The rock cathedral
Reminds me of the sea breezes
Of Stradbroke
And the reed flute seems
To be capturing the scene.
The slippery earth stone floor

Takes me back to mud sea flats,
Where seaweeds communicate with oysters
Fish and crabs.
Have you travelled all this way
To remind me to return home?

Uluru, your resting place in Australia,
Will not be the same without you.

I shall return home,
But I'm glad I came.
Tell me, my Rainbow Spirit,
Was there just one of you?
Perhaps, now I have time to think,
Perhaps, you are but one of many guardians
Of earth's peoples,
Just one,
My Rainbow Serpent,
Spirit of my Mother Earth.

Notes
The Rainbow Serpent is the Australian Aboriginal peoples' Mother of Life spirit.
She is also their Earth Mother spirit. She plays a dual role and she is also one.
Dreamtime – the time before life, as we know it, began.
Stradbroke – Stradbroke Island, off the coast of Brisbane, Queensland, Australia.
Uluru – Altar of the Australian Aboriginal peoples' Dreamtime. Sleeping and
resting place of their spirit, the Rainbow Serpent. Also known as Ayers Rock.

Oh Trugganner!

Oh Trugganner,
I weep for you,
For Lanney and all your race,
As I read Ryan's damning thesis
After one hundred years.
Your desperate guerilla warfare
Failed to oust the white foe,
And spilt blood and tears
Freely flowed
Over your much loved land.
Your race
Was the trophy sought
By the 'Christian, civilised' man
Who carried his depravities
Even beyond the grave.
Oh Trugganner,
I feel deep pain and sorrow
For the life he made for you.
What did you feel
When the foreign Doctor of Science
Stole like a thief in the night to the morgue
To cut from his body
Lanney's not yet cold head and his hands
In the name of 'Christian' science?
Oh Trugganner,
What did your dreamtime spirit feel
As it watched them take you after death

As a rare museum piece,
To stay forever
Under the rude stares
Of vulgar public gaze?
Oh Trugganner,
Destined to be
Not just the last of your race,
But a prized specimen for science too.

Oh Trugganner,
Let your restless spirit
Bring comfort to us all.

Give us wisdom and strength,
For we have not yet found ourselves
In this now alien land.
This land we thought was ours for ever,
Now peopled with racists,
Murderers, manipulators,
Who know too well the art
Of conquer, enslave, kill and destroy.
Oh Trugganner,
Let your spirit rise from the foreign museum
And walk with us in our grief.
In our once loved Native land,
The love that sustains us,
Is what our race was

Before the invaders came.
Oh Trugganner,
As you cried in the past,
So too now do your people cry
And have cried for the last two hundred years.
Oh Trugganner,
Will the dreamtime spirits of our race
One day rise with us
As they did with you,
To the whispering sounds of stalking feet
With our guns in our hands
And an ambush plan
The nullas, the spears and stones?
Or will we in servitude,
Die like you?
And will 'modern' scientists rave and drool
Over our bones
As they 'religiously' did
With Lanney and you?
Oh Trugganner!

Kiltara-Biljara* (Eagle Hawk)

For Den Boy

You came to me in your ninth year!
I looked and saw a tired, hurt
Forty-year-old man.
Your eyes bore the pain
Of rejection and sorrow.
I turned away, unable to meet your eyes.
I fought to find the lost child within you
And belated knew, the child was never there.
In spite of all the pain
You trod the survival path.
Unfolding daydream wings
You flew high in the sky
Rejecting your Mother Earth.
Like the eagle, free and proud and strong,
You took as your domain the sky.
I watched your wings grow stronger
And when you were fifty-five, going on thirteen,
You took to the air, for better, for worse,
And soared like the eagle tribe,
Refusing to travel no tracks, but your own.
You wanted to accept my love
But dared not take it.
Your experience of rejection
Still lingered in your heart
And warned you to accept no love

* The Barkendji (Mildura) tribal word for Eagle Hawk

No matter how freely given.
Love hurts too much
And you are battle-scarred
From too many rejected loves.
Soar
Little boy, old man!
Soar to the highest places.
Take care to rest in trees
Where crocodiles roam
You'll be safe and happy there,
Crocodiles can't climb trees.

I'll miss your going.

Mongarlowe

(Written at Judith Wright's place)

Oh Virgin Earth
I hear your cries of pain
As you toss and turn,
Denying me
My much needed sleep.
Ravished by man's rape
In the ugly past,
He left you
Bleeding, gasping,
Causing you
To menstruate
Out of time.
Gum trees twist and turn,
Sadly shedding eucalypt tears,
Which merge with your spilt blood
Seeping, souring your tormented soul.
A lubra wails by the creek.

Ghastly monuments
To your lost virginity.

Leave Straddie Unabridged

The serpent glides her way
Painfully and methodically
Over the glistening sands,
Making her way across the island
Of Minjerribah.
Her human animals stand and stare,
Feeling her sorrow and pain.
Gulls dip and swoop overhead,
Crying their mournful cry,
The shadow of the bridge
Etched clearly in the minds of all.
Sea snipes run from wave to wave
Searching for food and calling,
'Why this! Why this!'
The gulls' calls come sadly and clearly,
'The bridge spells doom for us all!
Doom for us all!
Write it in the sands of Time!
Write it in the sands of Time.'

The Rainbow Serpent sighs,
Meditating
The folly of man.

Custodians of the Land

On 22 April 1989 Oodgeroo of the tribe Noonuccal received an honorary doctorate from the Humanities Faculty of Griffith University. The following is the speech she gave when she received the award. It was written conjointly by Oodgeroo and Kabul.

Members of Griffith University, Honoured Guests and Friends. Allow me to begin this address by expressing my sincere gratitude to the Griffith University for bestowing such an honour upon me. It represents a milestone in the history of this land, now known as Australia, for it recognises (belatedly though it be) the value of a most ancient earth culture to modern society.

To the Aboriginal people, the modern history of this land began two hundred years ago, when the sacred shores of my people became the dumping ground for the 'undesirable elements' from the crowded and depleted lands and social order of Old England. Some of these castaways were perpetuators of inhuman and irrational studies in the evolution of species (including the human), who merrily continued their insane traditions of racial and class discrimination here. Naturally, the first to suffer under this fascism were the traditional owners and occupiers of Australia, the Aborigines.

There were many reasons why the colonists' considered Aboriginal people to be lesser creatures than apes. There were the obvious things, like our nakedness and different standards of physical beauty, but there was also their greed-based refusal to give credence to and therefore comprehend a non European-earth-raping culture, which, through an ancient excellence in social engineering, was not only highly successful but superior to their own.

We 'pagans', who had believed in and comfortably maintained our own strict 'code of moral behaviour' for all of our people for many thousands of years before the white man's culture was born, were soon to learn that the equivalent order, in their brave new world, was most sadistically maintained with the rabid and obsessive use of the infamous 'cat o' nine tails' whip.

We need not labour these things for the purpose of this event, except, perhaps, to take note and to remember that these basic living differences between the two cultures created a fundamental clash then, and the modern issue is one of diametrically opposed philosophies that continue to clash now. Blind prejudice to cultural difference is still being liberally indulged in today in this land now known as Australia.

Australia is still being used as a dumping ground for many other world cultures. Unfortunately, instead of providing a bridge between Aborigines and European Australians, it merely adds to the rift. It must be clearly understood that the Aboriginal nation (yet to be recognised) has little or no enthusiasm for the so-called multicultural society of Australia, for it is unbelievable and a great indictment of European Australians that the Aboriginal people find themselves once again at the bottom of the Australian socioeconomic scale with regard to multiculturalism. In the multicultural case, we continually find ourselves firmly lacking in any priority of position on any 'ethnic' shopping list. This is true in all areas, including theatre. But then again, one must never mention the selling off of the Aborigines' stolen lands to multinationals in the same breath as the expression 'multiculturalism'.

As a proud Aborigine, I have witnessed, among Asian and European peoples, the replanting of their grassroot cultures on my Aboriginal homeland, and I have seen only the continuation of prejudice and suffering for my people. Only the history of the European and English Australian, it seems, repeats itself over and over again in this, my country.

Modern Australia, however, does have the key to logical race relations, but White Australia is preventing it from happening. Firstly, it is prevented with egotistic insistence on assimilation for all other cultures, by implementing heavily weighted Anglo-Saxon educational methods and systems. Secondly, through refusing to acknowledge that traditional Anglo-Saxon estimations of what constitutes intelligence and criteria for assessing ability and achievement must be reshaped in order to recognise and include other aptitudes at grassroot level.

It is possible to rectify this situation with a sensible, fair and reasonable approach to education. Education departments must revise their out-of-date, mid-Victorian criteria. When tutors from other countries and Aboriginal elders from this country, through cultural exchange, are recognised and their true worth recognised in universities and schools, then we will have, and will be able to boast of, a truly multicultural society.

At present, however, when Aboriginal people 'achieve' at a university or tertiary institution, they are forced to lead a double life. By day such a person is a replica of a white Australian, slightly — sometimes heavily — suntanned, who is taught to respect and accept the same Anglo-Saxon heroes as his or her peers; by night, a 'real' person, with his or her own cultural identity. I have named this double existence. 'the super-hero syndrome'.

There are many Aboriginal people in Australia leading this double existence who are irreparably damaged by the static they receive from their own families and communities for their achievements in the Anglo-Saxon world. Their strivings are seen as betrayal and psychologically ill. They are known to their people as 'Jackys' and 'Marys', or 'coconuts', the definition being 'brown on the outside, white on the inside'. The reason for all this cattle dust is that the Australian heroes are all Anglo-Saxon, and if any Aboriginal student challenges this, she or he is frozen out of the education system until they learn to be 'rational'. Becoming 'rational' of course means 'agreeing to assimilate'. It is this or become the black dropout, those Aboriginal subjects of innumerable university theses and government surveys, the conducting of which regularly provides non-Aboriginal students with their own degrees.

European Australians must let go of England. It is time to do just that. American universities are the leaders in providing cultural role models for students. The way to a 'real' multicultural society in Australia is through providing relevant role models for our students. We must duplicate the American pattern, for it does work; I have seen it. Or must I, as an Aboriginal elder, advise Aboriginal students to seek higher education in America?

Australian educational institutions can and must lead the way in forcing parliaments to recognise these urgent needs. Concurrently, our universities must acknowledge and recognise the fact that their domineering and entrenched elitism still implements the mid-Victorian attitude of 'survival of the white tribe at any cost' and is counter productive to a racial equality of the future.

It is, therefore, both logical and imperative that this elitism be hastily dissolved. White Australians must accept that it is time for them to be the listeners and the learners. They must accept that Aboriginal and ethnic people have their own traditional and contemporary tutors, and they are available here and now. In short, let us learn and understand logical grassroot culture of *all races* — an exchange where *all races* stand equal unto each other. Then and only then can there ever be a true multicultural Australia.

But let us consider for one moment the reality of what is happening in this world today in racial terms. There can be no doubt that the grassroot peoples of the Southern Hemisphere are embarking on a natural course of balance. This is to be expected and accepted (if we are clever), after hundreds of years of evil and ugly colonial yoke. There can also be no doubt that in some cases, as in South Africa, where the rule of a fanatical white minority, using Christianity as their motive, anthropology as their weapon and technology as their alibi against the traditional land owners, can end only in the most dreadful letting of blood, the like of which we have not seen since the last World War. I need not spell out the similar patterns emerging in South America. Fiji, however, is a very real beginning of the Southern Hemisphere of the future, if indeed there is to be a future for humankind under the umbrellas of nations who have at their heads fascist, nationalist boys who long to play with atomic toys.

Reading between the lines, Vanuatu, New Caledonia, New Guinea, and the Torres Strait Islands will surely follow the trend that Fiji has set in the push for grassroot autonomy, the natural balance.

The Anglo-Saxon world is shrinking; the grassroot worlds are reawakening from the effects of the colonial brutality. Where, then, does this leave seventh-generation Australians? At present we have a situation where grassroot peoples are on one side and European and ethnic races in this country are on the other side. The predicament can easily lead to placing the Australian-born seventh-generation community in a proverbial hotseat with regard to their perpetuation of cruelty, apathy and violence towards the Aborigines, the grassroot custodians of this land.

But let us make no hasty mistake when pondering this natural, long-awaited and coming shift of the Southern Hemisphere. Grassroot autonomy in every sense, that is, economically, culturally, socially and psychologically, is the only path to racial harmony. And on this basis it is time to start drawing up a blueprint for the global village of the future. We of the Pacific must provide the working model of socioeconomic equality for all peoples.

There is no doubt that education, correctly applied, can meet our future needs in this, and recognition and acceptance of the true value of grassroot and ethnic teaching methods is a step in the right direction for an evenly balanced future.

This blueprint should begin, perhaps, with the establishing of the armed neutrality of Australia. We have lost too many sons and daughters to the war games their war lords play. An armed but neutral major power in the Southern Hemisphere must cause new thought, which will lead to new socioeconomic reform. New generations of non-violent, non-racist non-conformers will have the opportunity to uphold peace in the Southern Hemisphere. The dumping of war lords from other countries onto our shores, be they English, Japanese, South African, Chinese, German or any other, will turn the Australian multicultural dream of the nineties into the nightmare of the next century.

As I have previously stated, Australian history books assert that Aboriginal and Australian history began in 1770. Our children's textbooks still imply this nonsense. We are also urged to believe that our Aboriginal political existence began on 27 May 1967, with the referendum.

Australian archaeologists are just now beginning to discover what Aboriginal people have always known. We have been here for a very, very long time, and, furthermore, much to the disgust of some, have no intention of going away, even in the face of attempted genocide.

Our ancient history is locked in a cultural memory, which in turn is locked in the Alcheringa, or, as it has been re-named (incidentally, without our permission), the Dreamtime. Non-Aboriginal Australians will eventually receive this history, for it will be translated into forms that all can understand by the Aboriginal people themselves. This not only for our benefit, though we sorely need it, but also for the benefit of all races — this in spite of the fact that the present Constitution of Australia gives little to Aborigines in terms of cultural survival.

In the meantime, however, we must rely on our white friends to report our history from their perspective. Two educative books stand out in my mind — belatedly written, but of great importance. They should be used as textbooks at all levels of education from universities down. They are: *The Law of the Land*, by Henry Reynolds, and *The Fatal Shore*, by Robert Hughes.

These books are but two of a great mass of research emerging that will, in my view, change the very way this country thinks. In my opinion, they have the potential to represent the beginning of a new and great Australian philosophy - one that has no time or patience for the convenient prejudices of the self-indulgent and illegitimate squatocracy that has been the very meaning of the word 'Australia' for two hundred years. This new thought means most to the *young* Australians and is bringing them fascination with and pride in Aboriginal culture and less shame and guilt in their own. These two books also symbolise, for me, the great anger and bitterness that young Australians are feeling against an education system that has deliberately kept them blinded to the truth of the so-called 'bringing of civilisation' to this land. *Aboriginal activists will not forge change* and redress injustices as much as the young *white Australian* people, who are already outraged at being isolated from the deep wells of wisdom that dot the landscape of an ancient and profound culture.

The authors of these two books I have mentioned are in no way anarchists or revolutionaries; they are as academic, levelheaded and analytical as their families always hoped they would be. They have simply begun a sensible and logical step in this country's history by exposing past untruths, discovering the reality, assessing this and restating the facts intelligently.

I cannot praise these and other works of this kind too highly. Perhaps, when such ideas are introduced into our education systems, the present-day students may encourage their, what I call, 'mentally constipated adults' to also peruse these works.

You have heard the Aboriginal point of view. Before summing up I would like to introduce you to a non-Aboriginal point of view ... Last year you honoured Judith Wright McKinney with a doctorate. She is, in my opinion, the greatest poet of her generation. Here is the poem she wrote in her attempt to sum up 'White Australia'. What she has to say is worthy of your consideration.

Two Dreamtimes
(For Kath Walker)

Kathy my sister with the torn heart,
I don't know how to thank you
for your dreamtime stories of joy and grief
written on paperbark.

You were one of the dark children
I wasn't allowed to play with -
riverbank campers, the wrong colour,
(I couldn't turn you white.)

So it was late I met you,
late I began to know
they hadn't told me the land I loved
was taken out of your hands.

Sitting all night at my kitchen table
with a cry and a song in your voice,
your eyes were full of the dying children,
the blank-eyed taken women,

the sullen looks of the men who sold them
for rum to forget the selling,
the hard rational white faces
with eyes that forget the past.

With a knifeblade flash in your black eyes
that always long to be blacker,
your Spanish-Koori face
of a fighter and singer,

arms over your breast folding
your sorrow in to hold it,
you brought me to you some of the way
and came the rest to meet me,

over the desert of red sand
came from your lost country
to where I stand with all my fathers,
their guilt and righteousness.

Over the rum your voice sang
the tales of an old people,
their dreaming buried, the place forgotten.
We too have lost our dreaming.

We the robbers robbed in turn,
selling this land on hire-purchase;
what's stolen once is stolen again
even before we know it.

If we are sisters, it's in this —
our grief for a lost country,
the place we dreamed in long ago,
poisoned now and crumbling.

Let us go back to that far time,
I riding the cleared hills,
plucking blue leaves for their eucalypt scent,
hearing the call of the plover,

in a land I thought was mine for life.
I mourn it as you mourn
the ripped length of the island beaches,
the drained paperbark swamps.

The easy Eden-dreamtime then
in a country of birds and trees
made me your shadow-sister, child,
dark girl I couldn't play with.

But we are grown to a changed world:
over the drinks at night
we can exchange our separate griefs,
but yours and mine are different.

A knife's between us. My righteous kin
still have cruel faces.
Neither you nor I can win them,
though we meet in secret kindness.

I am born of the conquerors,
you of the persecuted.
Raped by rum and an alien law,
progress and economics,

are you and I and a once-loved land
peopled by tribes and trees;
doomed by traders and stock exchanges,
bought by faceless strangers.

And you and I are bought and sold,
our songs and stories too
though quoted low in a falling market
(publishers shake their heads at poets).

Time that we shared for a little while,
telling sad tales of women
(black or white at a different price)
meant much and little to us.

My shadow-sister, I sing to you
from my place with my righteous kin,
to where you stand with the Koori dead,
'Trust none — not even poets.'

The knife's between us. I turn it round,
the handle to your side,
the weapon made from your country's bones.
I have no right to take it.

But both of us die as our dreamtime dies.
I don't know what to give you
for your gay stories, your sad eyes,
but that, and a poem, sister.

In summing up, I would like to restate that a multicultural society can only successfully occur in this country when seventh generation Australians recognise the Aboriginal culture. No change will or can occur until the theft of Aboriginal land and the attempted enslaving and slaughter are redressed and compensated. This Aboriginal land will never accept and will always be alien to any race who dares try enslave her. Aborigines will always be the custodians of their traditional lands, regardless of any other enforced law system, for the land is our Mother. We cannot own her; she owns us! Thank you!

Glossary

Alcheringa: The creation of the universe, the time known to most people as the Dreamtime or the Dreaming.

Aura: Traditional-living Aboriginal people believe that individuals possessing great knowledge and wisdom radiate with coloured light. A blue aura may mean great wisdom whereas a white aura may signify a higher level of wisdom, compared to a higher 'dan'. It is believed that the body reflects in colour its mental, physical and spiritual condition.

Biami: The Good Spirit. He is the sun. Although the name is fairly common to Aboriginal people, there are many different spellings.

Coolamon: A shallow vessel with curved sides, usually carved from hardwood. Sometimes ornately decorated with totemic designs, it is used for carrying everything from food to small infants.

Earth Mother: Aboriginal people believe that the earth is the mother of mankind, that humans are born of the land. Concepts of land possession, as in European culture and others, are entirely foreign to the Aboriginal people, who believe the land and man are inseparably linked forever.

Frog Tribe: All Aboriginal stories contain educative information about the environment which can assist in survival. In the creation story, the Frog Tribe reference teaches a way of finding water in a drought. In areas of extreme weather conditions, frogs will bloat themselves with water in the wet season and bury themselves in mud. When the waterholes dry up in the dry season, the animal lives underground on the ingested moisture in a kind of suspended animation. Hunters who find themselves in waterless areas can easily find a drink at a dried-up waterhole by digging up a frog, puncturing the stomach and drinking the water stored inside.

Fullas: This is a term familiar to most Australians and in general was a colloquial way of referring to a group of men; but in the development of an Aboriginal 'patois' of the English language, like a regional dialect, the term has taken on a wider meaning and refers to all people, not just males.

Gidday: A greeting or salutation familiar to all Australians. Widely used at any time of day to mean 'hello'.

Message sticks: A stick of communication bearing important universal symbols sent from one tribe to another.

Opal: Semi-precious gem of rich colours found mainly in central west Queensland.

Quandamooka: To the Noonuccal Tribe from the Minjerribah (Stradbroke Island), Quandamooka is the sacred water spirit of Moreton Bay (near Brisbane).

Rainbow Serpent: The mother of life to all Aboriginal tribes. As the story indicates, she is the spirit responsible for the colour and shape of the land we live in.

Sacred place/sacred site: Aboriginal people believe that the land is spiritually alive and that certain places (usually of extraordinary, natural beauty) are the resting places of the creator, the mother of life, the Rainbow Serpent. These areas command absolute respect from the Aboriginal people and, during regular visits to re-establish contact with the Earth Mother and the spirit world, traditional Aboriginal conservation customs are practised. For instance, movement and voice levels are kept to a minimum; the area is meticulously inspected; controlled burning and seed distribution are practised if necessary; and sacred paintings or carvings are ceremoniously retouched. This practice of retouching, as in the story, ensures that the spirits do not grow weak, and that they will continue to ply their good favour upon the people.

Totem: All Aboriginal tribes have creatures which are sacred to them. Animals special to a given tribe may not be hunted in any way, captured or eaten by that tribe, for these animals are considered to have been blood relatives since their Alcheringa. A Kangaroo man cannot eat a kangaroo, a Carpet Snake man cannot eat a carpet snake, and so on. It is believed that humans were once animals born of the Rainbow Serpent. She bestowed human form as a gift for keeping her law. The law that no man may eat of his totem is really pure conservation ensuring the survival of all species in a given area.

Uluru/Ayers Rock: The birth place of the Rainbow Serpent. Uluru is the living altar and symbol of creation for the Aboriginal people.

Biography

Oodgeroo of the tribe Noonuccal
Custodian of the land Minjerribah

On 3 November 1920, Kathleen Jean Mary Ruska was born on North Stradbroke, an island in Moreton Bay about 30 kilometres east of Brisbane, and the home of the Noonuccal tribe.

There were seven children in the Ruska family, and all spent some time at the Dunwich Primary School. At the age of 13, and as an Aboriginal with no future in the State Education System, Kath went into domestic service in Brisbane. She was rescued from that fate by the Second World War when she served in the Australian Women's Army Service.

Kath married Bruce Walker, a waterside worker in Brisbane, and had two sons, Denis and Vivian. She joined the Communist Party because it was the only political organisation that eschewed the White Australia Policy, but left the Party because it wanted to write her speeches!

The sixties — the years of freedom rides, the struggle for the right to vote and the Gurindji strike at Wave Hill — saw Kath become a prominent and persuasive figure as she wrote and spoke for Aboriginal Rights, perhaps following the path of her father who had been active in the struggle for award wages for Aboriginal peoples as early as 1935.

In 1964 her first volume of verse and the first by an Australian Aborigine, *We Are Going*, was published (with the encouragement of Judith Wright and the aid of a Commonwealth Literary Fund) by The Jacaranda Press. Her second volume, *The Dawn Is at Hand*, followed in 1966. The honest and outspoken poems gained immediate acceptance and they were to be the forerunners of a considerable output which includes short stories, speeches, paintings, drama and film.

The Civil Rights struggle of the 60s and 70s saw Kath active on many local, State and, later, National Committees. She was Queensland State Secretary of the Federal Council for the Advancement of Aborigines and Torres Strait Islanders, Secretary of the Queensland State Council for the Advancement of Aborigines and Torres Strait Islanders, and a member of the Queensland Aboriginal Advancement League.

During this time of heightened activity associated with pressure to amend Section 51 and repeal Section 127 of the Australian Constitution, Kath Walker was part of the delegation which presented the case for reform to Prime Minister Menzies. This lobbying led to one of the most important Constitutional reforms since Federation when, on 27 May 1967, 90 % of the Australian Electorate supported the proposed amendments.

Later she served on the Aboriginal Arts Board, the Aboriginal Housing Committee and was chairperson of the National Tribal Council and the Stradbroke Land Council. From 1972 she was Managing Director of the Noonuccal-Nughie Education Cultural Centre, as well as a remedial teacher at Dunwich School. She lectured at universities and colleges throughout Australia on subjects ranging from uranium mining to conservation and the environment to Aboriginal culture.

In 1969 Kath Walker was the Australian delegate to the World Council of Churches Consultation on Racism in London, bringing the plight of her people to overseas attention for the first time.

This was the beginning of many a foray into the world outside Australia. In 1972 she was guest lecturer at the University of the South Pacific in Fiji; in 1974 the official Australian envoy at the International Writers' Conference in Malaysia; in 1975 the guest of the PNG Government at the PNG Festival of Arts; and in 1976 delegate and Senior Advisor to the Second World Black Festival of the Arts held in Lagos, Nigeria (surviving a plane hijack on her way home).

In 1978-79 she won a Fulbright Scholarship and Myer Travel Grant to the United States of America and was Poet-in-Residence at Bloomsburg State College, Pennsylvania.

In these same years, almost as if it were a necessary antidote to travel, she established Moongalba, or 'sitting-down-place', a five-hectare piece of coastal bushland on North Stradbroke Island where archaeological evidence shows that her ancestors had been in occupation for over 20 000 years. There in her caravan she welcomed visitors of all ages and races.

For many Aboriginal and Islander children from the cities, this was their first experience of the natural way of life of their ancestors. For people of other races it was a rare insight into another culture. To date, over 28 000 children and adults have learned about Aboriginal foodgathering practices, participated in a revival of arts and crafts, and listened to Aboriginal story tellers, and by so doing have come to understand, and more particularly respect, the often fragile but sustaining interrelationships of Australian nature.

Kath was the subject of Frank Heiman's film *Shadow Sister* (1977) for which she received an International Acting A ward and membership of the Black Hall of Fame. In 1970 the first edition of her anthology *My People* (Jacaranda Press) was published, and she wrote of her childhood in *Stradbroke Dreamtime* (1972: Angus and Robertson). As well as being a writer she was also an artist in her own right. She illustrated her own book (*Father Sky and Mother Earth*, Jacaranda Press, 1981), and in 1986 a volume of her paintings (*Quandamooka: The Art of Kath Walker*) was edited by Ulli Beier and published by the Aboriginal Arts Council with Robert Brown and Associates.

The eighties also saw further travel. In 1985 she was a member of the Australia/China Council party which toured China, and poems written on this tour (*Kath Walker in China*) became the first collection written by an Aboriginal to be co-published by Australian and Chinese publishing houses and presented in Chinese and English.

In 1986, at the invitation of Secretary-General Gorbachev, she was a delegate to the International Forum for a Nuclear Free World for the Survival of Humanity held in Moscow. On her way home from Russia she lectured in New Delhi on 'Aboriginal Grass Roots Culture'. And somehow in the same year she managed to be both actor and script consultant for Bruce Beresford's film *The Fringe Dwellers*.

The eighties also saw Kath's close involvement with the Land Rights Movement, which culminated in despair when the Federal Labor Government refused to honour its promise to enact National Land Rights Legislation.

So Kath Walker became Oodgeroo of the tribe Noonuccal, custodian of the land Minjerribah. Many of her awards she retained - the Jessie Litchfield Award, the Mary Gilmore Medal, and the Fellowship of Australian Writers' Award. But in 1987, as a Bicentennial protest, she returned the insignia of the MBE (awarded back in 1970) to the Crown via the Governor of Queensland. Notwithstanding this action, Oodgeroo and her son Kabul (Vivian) were scriptwriters and producers for the Dreamtime story *The Rainbow Serpent*, which was a major feature of the Australian Pavilion at World Expo 88. The text of *The Rainbow Serpent* was subsequently published by the Australian Government Publishing Service.

1988 also was the year of the award of an Honorary Doctor of Letters from Macquarie University.

In 1989 Griffith University awarded her the degree of Doctor of the University, and 1989 saw the world premiere of *The Dawn Is at Hand*, a musical setting of a selection of Oodgeroo's poetry by Malcolm Williamson, the Australian Master of the Queen's Music. This symphonic chorale was performed in Brisbane by the Queensland Symphony Orchestra, soloists and the Queensland State and Municipal Choir.

Oodgeroo died in 1993.